THE SONGS OF DAVID OLNEY

Volume I

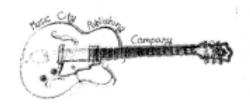

Nashville, Tennessee
(931) 433-1955
www.musiccitypublishingcompany.com

Design by Rachel Yellin Designs
Cover photo by Gregg Roth

ISBN: 978-1-5136-0042-0

August 2015

Manufactured in the United States of America on acid-free paper.

This book meets all ANSI standards for archival quality.

Table of Contents

Foreword

I first met David Olney 29 years ago. I had heard a tape of him singing "Stand Tall," and asked the club owner the name of the artist. I contacted David and asked him if the song had been recorded. He said that it had not but that he would be happy to give me a tape that he had made. Needless to say, I was taken by his generosity of spirit.

That began a friendship that has lasted nearly three decades. Over that time I've seen David create a body of work that is, to my mind, unparalleled. Please don't get me wrong, there are many singers and songwriters who write thoughtful, beautiful, and important songs that have moved me and many others. David, however, is in a class by himself.

David has been able to capture important moments from very unique perspectives. Who else has seen the crash of the Titanic as a love song or told the story of the entry of Jesus into Jerusalem from the perspective of the donkey? These are only two of the more notable contributions David has made to our understanding of the world around us. David's comments, which accompany the lyrics to each song, provide a fascinating look at the process by which he takes moments both large and small to create beautiful music.

Through it all, David has not forgotten that music exists to move and entertain. His songs are not moral or historical essays. Instead, they are stories and vignettes of life told in a way that at once gives us the opportunity to laugh, think, cry, question, and even dance. "Jama Ball" and "Walk Downtown" are important songs because they do not pretend to be important songs. They are just simply fun. Yes, we may feel for the lonely man at the bar who will, if he is so inclined, break into an Elvis impersonation. Certainly, we can all feel David's affection for his, "Rockin Little Jama Ball."

David's gift is his unique perspective on the world around us and his combination of intellectual curiosity and tenacity. In the years I have known David, we've had long discussions about everything from the origins of the First World War to the tragedies of Shakespeare. I have yet to find a subject about which David is not curious and informed.

It is sometimes easy, by focusing on the lyrics to David's songs, to forget their musicality. That would be a mistake. Each song is not simply a poem set to music. Rather, it is a seamless integration of the music and instrumentation to support the meaning and the feeling of each song and the lyrics become part of the music itself.

Undergirding all of David's work is a passion, not just for songwriting, but for understanding. It is an unbridled belief that the world around us is endlessly fascinating and deserving of attention. In many ways, it is this remarkable commitment that makes David the outstanding songwriter and performer that he is today.

This first collection of David on these lyrics merely scratches the surface of his body of work. I hope that there will be more to come. It is my great privilege to call David my friend and an honor to have been involved with this first volume of David's lyrics.

Jay Pilzer
Nashville, TN
July 2015

*Photo by Klaas
Jan Guchelaar*

Photo by Mary Sack

Introduction

When I was a kid, maybe 12 or 13 years old, every couple of weeks my mother would give me money to get a haircut. I would walk a couple of miles to an area of town called Fairlawn to Stanley's barbershop. I'd wait my turn reading the many sports magazines that were always on hand. Then Stanley would indicate that it was my time. I recall the smells of hair oil and shaving cream and aftershave that permeated the barbershop. And the mirrors all around that reflected one another and to infinity. This was the only place that I can remember seeing the back of me. It seemed somehow significant. Anyway, I'd hop up into the plush barber chair and Stanley would go to work. Buzz buzz. Clip clip. This routine had been going on for several years so whatever Stanley had to say to me or I to him of any import had been said a good ways back in the past. Now we spoke in minimalist language almost a code.

"The usual?"
"Yeah."
"Nice day."
"Yeah."
"How bout them Sox."
"Yeah."

Stanley always had his radio on, tuned to a local pop station that leaned toward the more temperate music of the day. A little Elvis, a little Chuck Berry, a good bit of bland white crap that passed itself off as rock, and a dose of Percy Faith, and a lot over the overwrought ballads of that era. The initial jolt of R&B, doo-wop, rockabilly, and whatever fit into the category of rock 'n' roll had subsided. Jerry Lee Lewis had been driven into exile, Buddy Holly was dead, and the next wave of great soul singers, led by Otis Redding and James Brown, had not broken loose. The folk boom had become nondescript. Music seemed to be lying dormant, waiting, waiting... But Stanley kept the radio on anyway – as background music, I suppose.

I should say here that, as a little kid, I was a big fan of the Lone Ranger. I thought he represented the way things ought to be, a model of Caucasian integrity. I did not explore the problematic relationship between the Lone Ranger and Tonto. Such weighty concepts were still in my future. I only saw his righteousness, his infallibility. This connection to the masked man later morphed into an appreciation of Perry Mason. Perry impressed me with his stoicism and his implacable collectedness in a deceitful world. These two men, the Lone Ranger and Perry Mason, were emblems of the white Anglo-Saxon Protestant ideal. Always above temptation, always unflappable in the face of danger. They never lost control of their emotions. They were never bamboozled. You never heard either one of them say," I love you beyond all comprehension" or, "holy shit, I didn't see that coming!" They were never overwhelmed by circumstances beyond their control. They were coldly perfect. And this, I had somehow accepted as the appropriate way to go at life.

Reality, however, was a different story. As I lurched and stumbled into adolescence and puberty, I found I was constantly bamboozled and overwhelmed. The sudden change in my attitude toward girls flummoxed me completely. Emotions flooded me with no warning:

anger, love, humiliation, elation, joy and sadness batted me about like a helpless ping-pong ball. All this and acne, too.

And then Ray Charles came on the radio one afternoon while I was having my hair cut at Stanley's barbershop. First, lush strings playing at an impossibly slow tempo and then raised voice. I was into it from the first note. Almost against my will. This was not rock. It was not aimed at the teen world. It was a grown-up singing to grown-ups about grown-up love and longing. In short, it was music my parents would like and that should have been poison to me. But it was not. The power of Ray Charles' singing rising above all differences in the world. Differences of age and race and gender and everything that dehumanizes all of us. All to express sadness and heartache. And yet it was not sad. It was triumphant! Not a triumph over sorrow but a triumph that allowed someone to accept sorrow as an important, maybe the most important, part of life. I couldn't move. I was paralyzed as Stanley snip snipped and clip clipped my hair.

Then it happened. "Coming out of the bridge." The road leads back to you," Ray's voice went unexpectedly into a falsetto. My head snapped back as if I had been punched in the teeth. This was a full grown man giving in to unabashed emotion. The cosmic tectonic plates shifted and the universe moved. Nothing would ever be the same. The Lone Ranger and Perry Mason were suddenly two pathetic bores. Life was not about conquering and controlling one's feelings but about experiencing them, pure and unadulterated. Oh, yeah!

I heard Stanley's voice like an alarm clock waking me from an intense dream. "What the hell are you doing? I almost cut your earlobe off!" I apologized and made it through the rest of the haircut without incident. Then I paid him and walked out of the shop into the wide, weird world.

So there it is. The reason, the meaning, the purpose. All for that moment of epiphany. That's why we play. That's why we sing. It's why I write songs.

David Olney
Nashville, TN
July 2015

Photo by Dan K. Reinli

Remarks on Chord Notations

This is a book of lyrics for songs that span David Olney's career. It is not a "song book" in that it does not include musical notation for the songs. We did include chords and some basics of how David plays them. Capo placement, or lack thereof, is noted for each song as are any deviations from standard tuning. The chords represent the shapes David is using and not what the chord actually is when a capo is used. For example, if the capo is on the third fret and David is using Em, G, and D shapes, those are the chord designations rather than Gm, Bb, and F.

When David tunes the sixth and/or first E string down a step, we note that as "tuned to D" with no capo.

Is this really John Barrymore or just someone
who thinks he's John Barrymore?
If he's really Barrymore,
Then the song takes place
in the '40s. If he is
someone deluded into
thinking he's Barrymore,
then the song could take
place today. In either
case, he is clearly more
of a romantic than the
bartender. I wanted to write a tango.
The guitar part is difficult for me to play
but I still give it a shot now and then.
It's a duet that's more of a
conversation. The song reminds
me of "The Great Gatsby."

Barrymore Remembers

Capo on second fret

Vamp on Em prior to lyric

Am   G   Am   G   Em
   Have I ever told you I was once quite the ladies' man?
           Bm   Em   Bm
My suits were Italian, my color vermillion
C   G   B   E
   My words soft as satin,   the language of love

My life was the movies and I was the leading man
The dashing romantic with a touch of the tragic
My profile was perfect and the language was love

    A
Yes sir, Mr. Barrymore, you must have been something back then
             D   E
They must have been wonderful years and they won't come again
    F#m   E
Yes sir, Mr. Barrymore, can I pour you another?

The women were lovely in the flickering Hollywood night
Of course, there was Garbo and Dietrich and Harlow
The look was come hither and the language was love

And my God! The parties. The nights were as bright as the days
The air smelled like honey, the stars shone like money
In the roar of the twenties the language was love

Yes sir, Mr. Barrymore, you must have been something back then
They must have been wonderful years and they won't come again
Yes sir, Mr. Barrymore, one more on the rocks?

This was a gay town as wild and as free as the night
We lived with abandon, we loved with a passion
We were storybook heroes in the language of love

But what was I saying? Where has everyone gone?
Quickly bartender, pour me another
Better make it a double, one more for the road
Yes sir, Mr. Barrymore, are you sure you can make it alright?
Yes the bar's closing down, call it a night

Recorded on "Ache of "Longing" and "Women Across The River"
Hayes Court Music/Irving Music

Chained And Bound To The Wheel

I got the tune for this from a song by Bland Simpson who I played with in New York a million years ago. The lyrics are a re-working of King Lear by Bill Shakespeare. If you're going to steal, steal from the best. Lear says "... I am bound upon the wheel of fire." The image stuck in my mind. There are

thousands of songs hidden in Shakespeare. The part, "Pardon me, let me introduce these friends of mine," sounds like Lear is introducing his rock band. "On guitar and vocals, a mournful fool with a holy line!" I wanted to capture some of Lear's madness and rage.

Chained And Bound To The Wheel

No capo

```
E           C       G           C       E
Excuse me, my friend but this is not where I want to be
         C       G           C       E
Is this the end? To be begging for some sympathy
         Am                  G           D
I've been out in the storm, I'm just looking to get warm
       Em          C       Am7         E
That's how it feels chained and bound to the wheel
```

Maybe you've heard they once used to call me King
It's only a word, only a word with a hollow ring
It was yesterday I gave it all away
There's no fair deal
Chained and bound to the wheel

```
Am
     Chained and bound
     G           D
Going up and coming down
          Am
Are you a dream? Are you real?
       G               D
If you can free me from this wheel
C    E
Do it now
Do it now
```

Pardon me, let me introduce these friends of mine
Let me see, here's a holy fool with a mournful line
Here's a man with no eyes, here's another in disguise
Only the mask is real
Chained and bound to the wheel

Recorded on "The Wheel"
Red Lilly Music/Sound Country Music

Covington Girl

Sergio Webb, John Hadley, and I wrote this one afternoon at John's place in Norman Oklahoma. Sergio was the driving force behind the music. I wanted to get some guns and bullets in the lyrics to play against the jauntiness of the melody. We got to the train robbery part of the song and I thought we were stuck because it would take too long to describe the logistics of stopping the train. John came up with:

"We rode and we rode to the top of the hill

Rolled a rock down the side of the ridge

It came to rest on the railroad tracks

Where the train came off the bridge"

He had stopped the train in four lines – brilliant. That's why John Hadley is John Hadley.

I love the mother in the tune telling her boys not to be late for dinner.

Covington Girl

Capo on second fret

C   Am
Billy put a bullet in the chamber of the gun, Bobby saddled up the bay
   C
A way over yonder the ten fifteen

Was rattling on its way, boys
       G   C
Rattling on its way

Mama said, Billy, keep your head on straight just get the money and ride
Bobby, you do like your big brother says
And I'll see you 'round dinnertime, boys
I'll see you 'round dinnertime

Am G   F   C   G
Life is grand with money to spend on anything in this world
   Am   G   F   C   G   C
A bonnet for Ma and a fiddle for Pa and a ribbon for my Covington girl, boys
                 G   C
A ribbon for my Covington girl

They rode and they rode to the top of the hill, rolled a rock down the side of the ridge
And it came to rest on the railroad tracks
Where the train comes off of the bridge, boys
The train comes off of the bridge

Billy held a gun on the railroad men, Bobby took a walk through the train
He took the rings from the women and the money from the men
And every gold watch and chain, boys
Every gold watch and chain

Life is grand with money to spend on anything in this world
A bonnet for Ma and a fiddle for Pa and a ribbon for my Covington girl, boys
A ribbon for my Covington girl

Recorded on, "Dutchman's Curve"
Red Lilly Music/Hadley Six Music/My Mexia Music

Deeper Well

This is the original version. Emmylou Harris recorded a version of "Deeper Well" on her "Wrecking Ball" album with additional lyrics she had come up with. She and producer Daniel Lanois had been working on the song in the studio and felt they were not nailing it. She called and asked if I minded if she wrote some words that reflected a woman's point of view more. I was honored that she was that deep into the song.

The song came out of a dream, in which I saw a woman standing next to a well holding a cup of water. She did not speak. I knew the water held some great mystical power. That was it. I woke up and wrote this song that day. Like a lot of my songs, I didn't know what I had until I played it in front of an audience. The pulse of the melody and the starkness of the words evoked a strong response.

Sometimes the song sounds to me like a blues song and sometimes like an Irish folk song. Then it starts to sound a bit Eastern European. I bet if you played it on the ukulele it would sound Hawaiian. I think Tuvan throat singers could really take it to another level.

Deeper Well

No capo
First and sixth strings tuned to D
Entire tune is in D modal

The sun burned hot it burned my eyes, burned so hot I thought I'd died
Thought I'd died and gone to hell looking for the water from a deeper well
So I went to the river but the river was dry, I fell to my knees and I looked to the sky
Looked to the sky and the Spring rain fell, I drank the water from a deeper well
Well well well well
I drank the water from a deeper well

Well I fell in love like a baby child, fell for a touch and I fell for a smile
Smile turned bitter and her touch turned cold, I could not keep what I could not hold
So I ran with the moon and I ran with the night and the three of us made a terrible sight
Whored and we gambled with the money we'd steal, looking for the water from a deeper well
Well well well well
Looking for the water from a deeper well

Well the moon got weak and he soon was gone and the night got sick and he died with the
dawn
Died with the dawn with a drink in his hand too sick to walk too drunk to stand
Time stood still but I ran wild and I got my fill with a crooked smile
Woke up on the floor of a jailhouse cell looking for the water from a deeper well
Well well well well
Looking for the water from a deeper well

The sun burned hot it burned my eyes, burned so hot I thought I'd died
Thought I'd died and gone to hell looking for the water from a deeper well
So I went to the river but the river was dry, I fell to my knees and I looked to the sky
Looked to the sky and the Spring rain fell, I drank the water from a deeper well
Well well well well
I drank the water from a deeper well

Recorded on "Deeper Well"
Hard Ball Music/Irving Music

Delta Blue

I was driving back to Nashville from New Orleans on Highway 61 (yes that Highway 61) straight through the Delta. It was just before sunset. A long cloud of smoke, coming from a source I couldn't see, hung over the trees on the horizon. I thought it might be ghosts from days gone by. Mississippi is a powerful place – you can feel it, joy and sorrow, love and hate. Robert Johnson and Muddy Waters, William Faulkner, and Jimmie Rogers.

I got help on this one from my friend Gwil Owen. This is one of the first songs of our now long-standing collaboration. He is a great songwriter and a dear friend.

Delta Blue

Capo on second fret

```
C        G7                        C
      The lazy river's always leaving town
G7                                 C
Claims tomorrow he's New Orleans bound
     F                      C     F
But he's not fooling me, it ain't true
       G7                          C
You know he'll never leave you, Delta Blue
```

The midnight train is rolling down the line
Trying to leave your memory behind
His whistle plays a low and lonesome tune
It's so hard to say goodbye Delta Blue

```
      G7                             C
Delta Blue, the stars are shining in the sky
      G7                          C  C7
Delta Blue, the Delta moon is in your eyes
      F                      C  F
You ask me if I love you, yes I do
      G7                      C
You know I always will, Delta Blue
```

I get a little older every day
Maybe I should make my getaway
But all it takes is just one look from you
You know I'll never leave you, Delta Blue

Recorded on "Omar's Blues"
David Olney Songs/Turgid Tunes

10

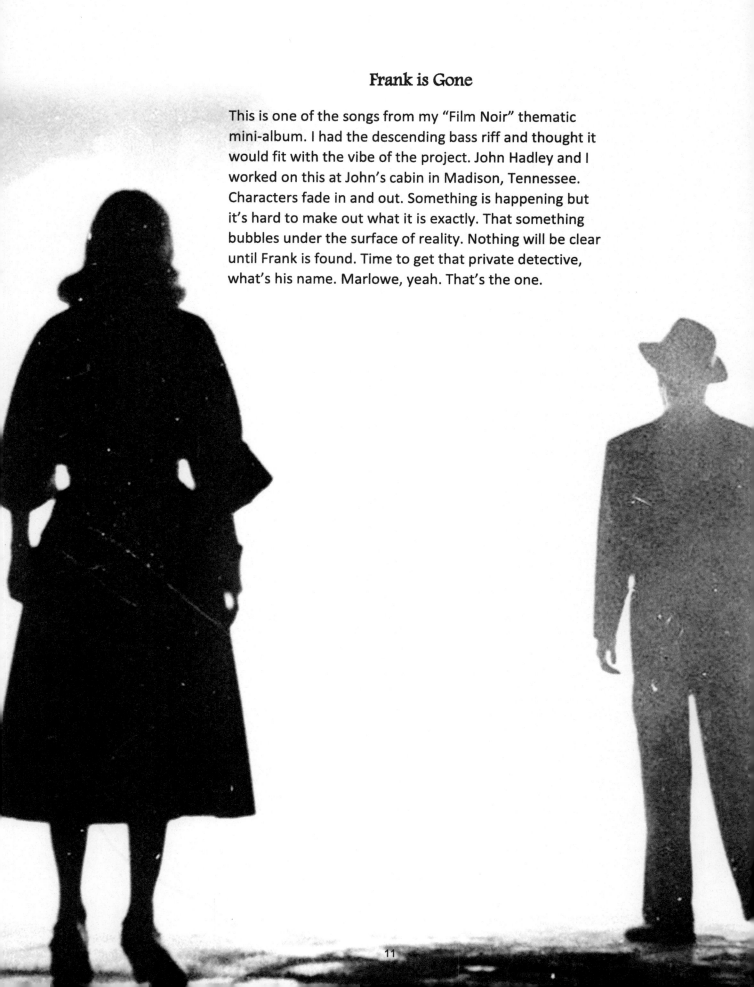

Frank is Gone

This is one of the songs from my "Film Noir" thematic mini-album. I had the descending bass riff and thought it would fit with the vibe of the project. John Hadley and I worked on this at John's cabin in Madison, Tennessee. Characters fade in and out. Something is happening but it's hard to make out what it is exactly. That something bubbles under the surface of reality. Nothing will be clear until Frank is found. Time to get that private detective, what's his name. Marlowe, yeah. That's the one.

Frank Is Gone

No capo
Verses are a repeated run:
  Low E, E octave, Eb, Bb, A, Eb, D, A, Ab, D, Db, G, F#, C, B

Downtown streets slick with rain
Watch your step, don't talk to strangers
Feel the rhythm on the track
Don't turn 'round, don't turn back

Am Bm C Bm Em
I can't stay here anymore, I've forgotten why I came
Am   Bm   C Bm
Some things are worth fighting for
Em   C7   B7
 Leave your number, leave your name

Gracie leaves the porch light on
She waits for Frank but Frank is gone
Frank is gone, he won't be back
Don't turn 'round don't turn back

(Yeah I know him, he's okay
 I think he left here yesterday
 Where'd he go? He went away
 Yeah, I know where but I can't say)

I can't stay here anymore, I've forgotten why I came
Some things are worth dying for
Leave your number, leave your name

Downtown streets slick with rain
(Yeah, I know him, he's okay)
Frank is gone, he won't be back
Don't turn 'round, don't turn back

Recorded on "Film Noir"
Red Lilly Music/Hadley Six Music

Go Down Dupree

This is a song from my "Dave Olney and the X-rays" days. It's a retelling of the old blues tune "Betty and Dupree" – which I first heard from Chuck Willis', "King of the Stroll." Chuck wore a turban on stage which is unspeakably cool. I recorded it on "Robbery and Murder, trying to catch the vibe of Eddie Cochran's "Summertime Blues."

Go Down Dupree

No capo
Lead in: Vamp in A, then A, G, A, A, G, A, A, D, A

A   A, G, A, D, A
Betty and Dupree had a love affair
A   A, G, A, D, A
Betty don't believe that Dupree care
  D   D,C,D,G,D
Dupree said, I love you, baby, that's the truth
A   A,G,A,D,A, A,G,A,D,A
Betty say, you got to show me some proof

Betty say she want a diamond ring and fifteen pearls on a golden chain
Give me a ruby that'll shine like the moon, bring 'em here, baby, and bring 'em here soon
She said
  G   D   A
  Go down, Dupree, go down
  G   A   A,G,A,D,A ,A,G,A,D,A
  Go down, Dupree, go down

Dupree went home and got a forty four then he walked on down to the jewelry store
He said to the man, I ain't here to play, give me your jewels before I blow you away

The man said, alright, but don't you do me no harm. Dupree never seen him hit the burglar alarm
He walked out of the store straight into the cops. He never had a chance so he just give up
And it's
  Go down, Dupree, go down
  Go down, Dupree, go down

Betty saw Dupree in the federal slam. He said, you're the reason I'm where I am
And it's ten long years 'fore they let me out. Betty said, don't cry, it's the thought that counts
She said
  Go down, Dupree, go down
  Go down, Dupree, go down

Recorded on "Robbery and Murder"
David Olney Songs/Three Minute Movie Music

If I Were You

This song seems so simple and yet, to me, it's very complex. As soon as you say, "if I were you..." it becomes murky as to who is being referred to. Is it me or you? Who would put a candle in the window, me or you?

In the song, love becomes the only thing that can be counted on. Musically, Ben E. King with The Drifters is the model. I got help from John Hadley on this one.

If I Were You

Capo on second fret
Sixth string is tuned down to D (without capo)

D
If I were you here's what I'd do
                        G
I'd put a candle in the window
                  D   A
I'd watch the clouds roll across a moonlit sky
     D
And while you were gone I'd carry on
                    G
And I'd dream of your returning
            D A   D
That's what I'd do   if I were you

If I were you I'd be as blue as the hills on the horizon
I'd keep my eyes on a day that's yet to come
I'd remember this place and your face
And the promise that we made here
That's what I'd do if I were you

     G
And if you were me you would see
                       D
Though the miles keep us apart
    G
And if you were me you would believe
                D
I will hold you in my arms again
           A
Not just in my heart

If I were you here's what I'd do
I'd put a candle in the window
That's what I'd do if I were you
That's what I'd do if I were you
That's what I'd do if I were you

Recorded on "Dutchman's Curve"
Red Lilly Music/Hadley Six Music

If My Eyes Were Blind

This is the song where I found my own voice as a writer. No one else could have written it. The language is from some time past and is somehow quirky. But it is me.

My friend, Russ Nelson, had been explaining entropy to me. Life is water flowing downhill and it ends in a standing pool that is oblivion. The energy it takes to live is always running out – – nothing lasts - the end. This seemed so unfair to me that I began searching for ways to beat entropy.

A month or so after my conversation with Russ I was asked to write a song for a wedding. "If My Eyes Were Blind" is what came out.

I had the tune and the first verse of the song. It was different from, and better than, anything I had written but I wasn't sure how to go forward. I decided to take a walk and clear my head. It was a beautiful Spring day. A block away I could see a little boy playing with his dog. His dad stood nearby, beaming. A car came around the corner and the dog ran in front and was hit. The boy was distraught, of course. The car immediately pulled over and the driver, a man in his thirties got out. The dad walked up to him looking very serious. Then they both moved to the dog lying in the street. At that point I was just walking past. It was incredibly sad and intense. I continued on since there was no way I could help. Five minutes later I decided to go back to that scene to see how it had ended. The dog was up and wagging his tail. Miraculously, he had only been stunned. The boy was beside himself with happiness. The driver and the dad were smiling and shaking hands. I made it back to my apartment and wrote the remaining verses to "If My Eyes Were Blind".

Love is the only thing that can conquer entropy.

If My Eyes Were Blind

No capo

```
Am                        F                        C
If my eyes were blind the darkest night could never hold a mystery
Am                    F                      C              G
If my eyes were blind I'd hold your features fast within my memory, within my mind
              Am
If my eyes were blind
```

Should my voice grow weak, only you could hear the voice inside me
Should my voice grow weak, never with a word would I deny thee
I would not speak, should my voice grow weak

Should my mind grow dim and innocent as on the day God made me
Should my mind grow dim, I'd love you like a child or a baby
I'd be gentle as a lamb should my mind grow dim

When my youth is gone, in my eyes you shall remain a beauty
When my youth is gone, in my ears I'll hear you singing sweetly the sweetest song
When my youth is gone

When my body dies darling, I could never leave you lonely
My spirit shall arise to comfort and to care for you only
To sympathize

```
              Am        G
When my body dies
                  Am        G
When my youth is gone
                    Am        G
Should my mind grow dim?
                    Am        G
Should my voice grow weak?
              Am
If my eyes go blind
```

Recorded on "Deeper Well"
Warner-Tamerlane Publishing

I'll Fall In Love Again

This has a kind of classical feel — — a stateliness. Tomi Lunsford sang the backup vocals which I think of as the lead instrument in the music. I asked her to listen to "Baby Mine" from the Disney movie "Dumbo". Betty Noyes sang the song in the movie. I wanted to get that sound. Tomi got it in spades.

I'll Fall In Love Again

No capo

Intro: C G 7 C

```
G7          C
I'll fall in love again
G7        C    Cdim    Em
One day I know I'll fall in love again
          Cdim           Em G    G7                    C
And the dark clouds will roll away and the world will be new again
E7                  Am      F    C G7        C    F   C    E7
My broken heart will mend     when I fall in love again
     Am              E7sus  E7      Am            E7sus  E7  Am
But, oh, the world is cold tonight, the wind cuts me in two
            Em              Am        Em      Am  G
One day I will be alright when the Springtime sun shines through
         G7            C          E7        Am      F
And the Spring rain will wash away my tears and my pain
     C G7          C   F  C
When I    fall in love again
```

Recorded on "Real Lies"
Hayes Court Music/Irving Music

Jama Ball

Jama Ball was a friend of mine from years back. She was beautiful and vivacious and funny and smart. And totally uninterested in me. But the name was too cool to pass up. I borrowed the melody from an old blues tune, "East St. Louis Blues," that was done by Blind Willie McTell and Furry Lewis among others. I had first heard the tune on a John Hammond Jr. record. My favorite verse:

"She's the gravy on my mashed potatoes

She's my little all in all

She's my conversation stopper

She is my rockin little Jama Ball"

Jama Ball

No capo

```
A                         E              D
What's the deal? Is she for real?  She's got me feeling 'bout ten feet tall
              A                    E              A  E A E A
That's why I'm telling everybody 'bout my rockin' little Jama Ball
```

Sometimes she's high, sometimes she's tight, sometimes she's low and away
But as long as she's with me anyway she be will be okay

```
D                              Adim
Man, you think you're something, but what you is is nothing
     A         E      A              F#m
Cuz what you got aint nothing at all
         F#m                          F
Feast your eyes on something fine, just remember that she's mine
           E                     Eaug
Keep your cotton pickin' fingers off my baby Jama Ball
```

She's the gravy on my mashed potatoes, she's my little all in all
She's my conversation stopper, she's my rockin' little Jama Ball

What's the deal? Is she for real? She's got me feeling 'bout ten feet tall
That's why I'm telling everybody 'bout my rockin' little Jama Ball

Recorded on "Top To Bottom"
Hayes Court Music/Irving Music

Jerusalem Tomorrow

"Man you should've seen me way back then,

I could tell a tale, I could make it spin."

That's how it started, those two lines. I wrote them down not knowing where they would lead. Whoever would say such a thing was someone who took pride in his ability to lie - a charlatan of some sort.

I had been watching a lot of reruns of "Gunsmoke" and tried to put the song in the Old West. A snake oil salesman selling worthless, high alcohol content "medicine" to the Dodge City rubes. But the story went nowhere. I was stuck. Somehow the snake oil salesman became a desolate, phony preacher but I couldn't see the plot. I moved the desert from the Old West to the Near East and something clicked. It wasn't 1870 Dodge City, but first century Judea.

The main character is an unnamed soul not out for money but for love; who never actually makes an appearance in the song. He is only talked about. The story does not end. We only know that they are heading for Jerusalem tomorrow.

If a true savior of the world, of whatever religion or non-religion, were to actually show up on Earth, would we be able to recognize him or her as the real thing?

"Christ's Entry Into Jerusalem" original painting by Debby Atwell

Jerusalem Tomorrow

Capo on second fret

```
Am                                    Dm      Am                        E
Man, you should have seen me way back then.  I could tell a tale I could make it spin
       Dm                      Am
I could tell you black was white, I could tell you day was night
   Am                  E
Not only that I could tell you why
                        Am
Back then I could really tell a lie
```

Well, I'd hire a kid to say he was lame, then I'd touch him and I'd make him walk again
Then I'd pull some magic trick I'd pretend to heal the sick
I was takin' everything they had to give
It wasn't all that bad a way to live

Well, I'm in this desert town and it's hot as hell, but no one's buyin' what I got to sell
I make my lame kid walk, I make a dumb guy talk
I'm preachin' up a storm both night and day
Everyone just turns and walks away

Well, I can see that I'm only wasting time so I head across the road to drink some wine
This old man comes up to me, he says, "I seen you on the street"
You're pretty good if I do say so myself
But the guy comes through here last month, he was somethin' else

Instead of callin' down fire from above, he just gets real quiet and talks about love
And I'll tell you somethin' funny, he didn't want nobody's money
I'm not exactly sure what this all means,
But it's the damnest thing I swear I've ever seen

Instrumental: Dm Am Am E Am

Well, since that time every town is the same, I can't make a dime I don't know why I came
I decide I'll go and find him and find out who's behind him
He has everyone convinced that he's for real
Well, I figure we can work some kind of deal

Well, he offers me a job and I say fine. He says I'll get paid off on down the line
Well, I guess I'll string along. Don't see how too much can go wrong
As long as he pays my way I guess I'll follow
We're headed for Jerusalem tomorrow

Recorded on "Deeper Well," "Live in Holland," and "The Stone"
Hayes Court Music/Irving Music

Johnson City Blues

Here's another song written with Sergio Webb and John Hadley. Our goal was to come up with something with a Doc Watson feel.

Whenever I'm in Johnson City, Tennessee, I feel like I've traveled, or somehow landed in a parallel universe. Like I'm suddenly in a work of fiction. If you don't live in Johnson City, it's the kind of place that makes you really want to go home. The last verse "… So play the one we used to play back when there was nothing else to do" reminds me of my days in Chapel Hill, North Carolina in the 1960s hanging out at the "Cats Cradle." That was the club started by a lovely

woman, Marcia Wilson, which became the hangout for Chapel Hill musicians. It was the center of my world back then. I met Tommy Goldsmith and Steve Runkle at The Cradle. They moved to Nashville a year before I did and both had a great influence on me. God bless The Cradle and Marcia Wilson.

Johnson City Blues

Capo on the second fret

```
Intro :D  E  G A D E D G A
D                    G
Thought I was heading home
A         D         G A
But I got turned around
D                        G
Something got a hold on me
A         D     G  A
Now I'm Carolina bound
G              Gsus  G
I don't want to talk   about
Gsus   G        F       A
Or think about the trouble I've been through
D
So raise a glass and sing a verse
A           D     G   A
Of those Johnson City Blues
```

Everything is looking up
As far as I can see
Nothing's going to bring me down
Even this rain feels good to me
So tell them all where I come from
I've packed my bags and shined up both my shoes
And I've had as much as I can stand
Of those Johnson City Blues

I'm heading cross the mountain
See what kind of heartache I can find
There's nothing here to hold me now
Nothing I can't leave behind
So play the one we used to play
Back when there was nothing else to do
But raise a glass and sing a verse
Of those Johnson City Blues
Those Johnson City Blues

```
Bb     C    D
```

Those Johnson City Blues

Recorded on "Robbery and Murder"
Red Lilly Music/Hadley Six Music/My Mexia Music

King of Soul

For me, Otis Redding was the King of Soul. I think Steve Cropper said that when Otis died, "even the tough guys cried." I imagine heaven is a place where fictional as well as real people go and mingle. Where Romeo and Juliet can meet Otis Redding. His music was so powerful and full of soul. "I've Been Loving You a Little Too Long" is church music in the truest sense. I saw a picture in a book of Otis' body being brought out of Lake Monona in Wisconsin. It triggered something inside me and I wrote this. Long live The King of Soul.

King of Soul

No capo

```
G  C  G  C  G  D  G  C  G
                    D       C          G       C                          G  D
Like a shooting star the plane went down      in dark and troubled waters
G      D      C       G          C              G  D      C
Did he call his true love's name?       Did he hear her answer?
                          G
The news came on the radio
 B                    Em   C      G          C      G        C          G
   Now every rock and roller knows      the king of soul is dead and gone
      D            G
Long live the king of soul
```

Romeo and Juliet pledged their love forever
They were just two teenage kids but their hearts burned with a fever
For love they lived and for love they died
For the love that won't grow old, for the love that trembles in the voice
Of the mighty king of soul, he's the mighty king of soul

```
C            G              B
He's my candle in the wind
               Em      C      G
He's my shelter from the cold
         C          G   C        G
He's my strength when I am weak
         D          G   C
He's the mighty king of soul
      D          G   C
Long live the king of soul
         G      D      G      C      G  D  G
He's the mighty king of soul
```

Recorded on "Deeper Well"
Hard Ball Music/Hayes Court Music/Irving Music

Lilly of the Valley

My daughter spells her name this way, so it is not a mistake on my part, but on hers. I wanted to try and catch the feel of a Carter family song - a sort of "American - Victorian" formality to the lyrics. "Wildwood Flower" has that quality. I recorded it with a friend, A.C. Bushnell, on old timey fiddle. He keeps the song from getting too proper. The Carter Family made a real impression on me. Maybelle's guitar playing is still the standard. She and Sarah and A. P. became huge stars in their day and yet they stayed connected to their Clinch Mountain roots in an almost mystical way. Their songs are both forceful and gentle - shy and forward - full of sorrow and full of joy. That's what I was going for.

Lilly of the Valley

Capo on second fret

C   G7
Down the mountains through the valley runs a river deep and wide
                             C
I can see her 'cross the water over on the other side
                          G7
She is smiling, she is laughing as she waves her hand to me
                                      C
She's my Lilly of the Valley from the state of Tennessee

When the wintertime is over and the season turns to Spring
In the fields of greenest clover I will hear the robin sing
The dogwoods will be holding forth In all their majesty
For my Lilly of the Valley from the state of Tennessee

           F   C
She's my Lilly of the Valley From the state of Tennessee
           F   C   G7
She's as pretty as a princess in her fancy finery
           C   G7
When she puts her arms around me it means all the world to me
                                      C
She's my Lilly of the Valley from the state of Tennessee

Bluebonnets grow in Texas, they are lovely I am sure
But when I'm with my Lilly I could long for nothing more
The moon, the sun, the stars that shine in heaven's gallery
Love my Lilly of the Valley from the state of Tennessee

She's my Lilly of the Valley from the state of Tennessee
She's as pretty as a princess in her fancy finery
When she puts her arms around me it means all the world to me
She's my Lilly of the Valley from the state of Tennessee

Recorded on "Through a Glass Darkly"
David Olney Songs

Little Bird (It's What I Do)

Written in the shadow of Mount Chocorua in Tamworth, New Hampshire. The little bird sings as the winter wind howls. They are just doing what they were created to do. The anyone in the last verse is borrowed from e.e. cummings "anyone lived in a pretty home town." I think of the song as a kind of mission statement for my life. Every now and then I get a glimpse of what a remarkable thing it is to be alive and breathe this holy air.

Little Bird (It's What I Do)

Capo on third fret

Am
Little bird, Little bird
Dm   Am
High up in the tree
Little bird, Little bird
E7   Am
Why do you sing to me?

    Am
    It's what I do and what I do
     Dm   Am
    I do all summer long
    Dm   Am
    I'm a little bird
 E7   Am
    This is my song

Winter wind, Winter wind
You howl and you moan
Winter wind, Winter wind
And chill me to the bone

It's what I do and what I do
I do all winter long
I'm the winter wind
This is my song

Anyone, anyone,
Every anywhere
Born into this precious life
To breathe this holy air

It's what I do and what I do
I do my whole life long
This is who I am
This is my song

It's what I do and what I do
I do my whole life long
This is who I am
This is my song
Recorded on "When the Deal Goes Down"
Red Lilly Music

Love's Been Linked To The Blues

I recorded this at Cowboy Jack Clements' studio with Jim Rooney and Tommy Goldsmith producing. Stephanie Davis played the trumpet. I was then playing in a trio with Stephanie on fiddle and trumpet and Mike Fleming on bass. This is one we did. A slinky kind of blues with a world-weary attitude. I had come to the conclusion that everything I enjoyed was bad for my health.

Love's Been Linked To The Blues

Capo on third fret
Intro: Vamp between A7 and Em7

```
         A7            Em7         A7            Em7
It was in the morning paper, in the evening paper, too
      A7        Em7    A7      Em7     A7
And I saw it on TV      so I know it must be true
      D7          Am7           D7              Am7
This ain't no idle rumor, they've got the cold hard facts
        A               Bm7    C#m7        Cm7
In the lab they checked it out   on little mice and rats
        E7                        D7
Just in case you haven't heard I'll give you the bad news
A         Cm7     Bm7  A        E
Love's been linked to the     blues
```

You start out feeling happy but then love brings you down
You're acting like a hero, you wind up like a clown
In study after study it's the heart that gets broke
They're working 'round the clock searching for the antidote
It's true that it's sad but it's sadder that it's true
Love's been linked to the blues

So you've got to be real careful and always on your guard
Falling in love is harmful to your heart
It's worse than they suspected, it's as bad as it gets
The Surgeon General says you're better off with cigarettes
If you must have your bad habits why don't you stick to booze

```
A         Cm7     Bm7    C#m7    Cm7
Love's been linked to the       blues
    E                       D7
It's true that it's sad but it's sadder that it's true
A         Cm7    Bm7  A7
Love's been linked to the blues
```

Recorded on "Roses"
Hayes Court Music/Irving Music

My Lovely Assistant

Another song I wrote with my friend, John Hadley. I was on my way out to his cabin in Madison and was worried that I didn't have a single idea for a song. A van passed me on the highway and on the side was written "Zambini Cleaners." I don't recall what it was they cleaned, but I was taken with the name Zambini. The "Great Zambini," I thought, "Master Magician." He could make anything disappear but a broken heart. Who broke it? His lovely assistant, of course. John and I worked it through over the course of a day. On the recording for my CD "Migration" that's John saying "Silence! I must have silence!"

My Lovely Assistant

No capo

```
E              Ebdim      E
Good evening, ladies and gentlemen
         Ebdim   E                    Ebdim      E
Welcome one and all to an evening of magic and mystery
         Ebdim        E
In this truly magnificent hall
    F#m       C#7    F#m                C#7      F#m
Say hello to my lovely assistant, she'll mesmerize with her look
           C#7      F#m               C#7      F#m     A7
She taught this master magician the oldest trick in the book


D                  A        D              A
Love is the ultimate mystery, love is its own crystal ball
   D              A        E          A        E
Love is the perfect illusion, it's really not magic at all
```

But enough of this idle chatter
Let us get on with the show
We'll begin this evening's performance with a trick I don't think you know
Keep your eye on my lovely assistant as she rips my heart from my sleeve
And turns it into confetti and throws it back at me

Love is the ultimate mystery, love is its own crystal ball
Love is the perfect illusion, it's really not magic at all

Silence! I must have silence, not a sound to be heard in the room
Now watch as my lovely assistant steps into "The Grim Box Of Doom"
I'll pierce it with razor sharp daggers
You'll scream, you'll cry, you'll gasp
You'll cringe as I crank up the chainsaw and methodically cut her in half

Love is the ultimate mystery, love is its own crystal ball
Love is the perfect illusion, it's really not magic at all

Recorded on "Migration" and "Lenora"
Red Lilly Music/Hadley Six Music

Oh My Love

Here's another "X-Rays" era song. Whenever I get writer's block, I try to write a song Buddy Holly might have liked. Simple and direct with a driving melody. The gist of the lyric is: they say we can't but we're going to anyway because we're in love and they are stupid. Teens against parents, lovers against the world. The way it ought to be.

Oh My Love

No capo

```
G           D              G
Oh my love hear me as I call to you
                    D                      G
I offer my hand. It seems like the right thing to do
      C              G      D                    G
And I offer this heart full of pain, it'll bring you more tears than the rain
                          D           G
The rain's not much but it's the best I can do
```

Our hearts are young, there's a light of love in our eyes
But in times like these it's so hard for love to survive
And I see how you're looking at me, you need more than just sympathy
Sympathy's not much but it's the best I can do

```
C         D
Oh oh oh oh oh oh
G
Oh my love
C         D
Oh oh oh oh oh oh
G         D
Oh my love
```

The day is done, see the stars how they shine
Oh my love how I wish they were mine
For it won't be a moment too soon when I give you the stars and the
moon
The moon's not much but it's the best I can do

I've heard them talk and say that I'm bound to fall
I've seen them smile and act like they don't know me at all
They say that our love cannot grow. Tell me what do they know?
They don't know much if that's the best they can do

Oh oh oh oh oh oh
Oh my love
Oh oh oh oh oh oh
Oh my love

Recorded on "Contender"
Mighty Mighty Music

One Tough Town

I dreamed up a fellow, Slats Blatvic, a Vaudeville comedian. A song and dance, pie in the face kind of guy. In 1922, he is already past his prime. The one night stands, the unamused audiences, the booze and all the rest are catching up with him. One night after a show in Baltimore, Slats is abducted by aliens. And I mean beings from outer space. He is taken to their planet and, much to his amazement, he is asked to teach these creatures about comedy. They are advanced enough to have mastered space travel, but are painfully aware that they have no sense of humor. They figure Slats can get them up to speed. Slats spends his remaining years on his adopted planet revered by all. He writes his autobiography and calls it, "Earth, One Tough Town."

One Tough Town

Capo on second fret

A
I've been all around this universe
                                    A7
I've seen the best, I've seen the worst
D7
You know the circuit, I've really worked it
A   D7 A   D7   A
I'm telling you I've been around
     E   D7
The dives and the big joints, they all have their good points
     A   D7   A   E
But Earth, that's one tough town

Anywhere else my routine just kills
It's top shelf a-one material
It's subtle, it's magic, it's true, it's fantastic
So why on Earth does it bring them down
I don't know and I don't care but I'll never go back there
Earth, that's one tough town

     D7   A
They take you to the judge and they try you
         D7   A
Then they take you out back and crucify you
       C#7   F#m
They put a hole in you you could drive a truck through
     B   E7
And holler, "If you can't take a joke then..."

If you're thinking about getting into the biz
I can show you where it's at, I can tell you what it is
I'll show you my joke book
Go ahead, take a good look, but grab a pencil and write this down
If you do you'll regret it, you better just forget it
Earth, that's one tough town

Recorded on "One Tough Town" and "Live at Norm's River Road House, Vol. 1"
Red Lilly Music

Roll This Stone

From my CD "When the Deal Goes Down." It started out as a take on the myth of Sisyphus but turned into a rant from a farmer circa 1900. He is a person who stands alone and keeps his thoughts to himself - once an American archetype. That person has been replaced by the team player: "the company man" who doesn't make waves. I miss the old guy. That's the fellow in the song. He knows he's going nowhere, but that's okay as long as he keeps his independence.

Roll This Stone

No capo

```
A           E           A
I'm gonna roll this roll this stone
                                E
I'm gonna roll this roll this stone
A           G
I'm gonna roll this roll this stone
      D                   F
Don't want your help, I wanna do it alone
A       E           A
I wanna roll this roll this stone
```

I'm goin' to the top from the bottom to the top of the hill
I'm goin' to the top from the bottom to the top of the hill
I'm goin' to the top from the bottom of the hill
I don't care if it gets me killed
I'm gonna roll this roll this stone

```
D                   C           A
Me and this mule gonna plow this cold hard ground
   D                   C       E
Til me and this poor old mule both fall down
```

I'm gonna dig a hole so deep I can't get out
I'm gonna dig a hole so deep I can't get out
I'll dig a hole so deep I can't get out
When I get to the bottom, gonna jump and shout
I'm gonna roll this roll this stone

Recorded on "When the Deal Goes Down"
Red Lilly Music/Hadley Six Music

42

Roses

I started "Roses" in a motel in St. Louis. I was worn out from the road and discouraged with life in general. I guess I felt I needed a miracle. Since none seemed to be forthcoming, I made one up. An ancient oak tree is struck by lightning. Instead of being destroyed, the oak blossoms roses. I worked on the song over the next couple of days and finished it in a room at the Lincoln Park Inn in Chicago.

When I'm repeating "roses, roses, roses…" at the end of the song, I see a street vendor in New Orleans selling flowers.

Original painting by Rik van Iperen

Roses

No capo

Em   D   C   D
Lightning spoke to the Wind
   Em   D C   D
The Devil's in me today, my friend
       Em   D   C   D
Do you see that old Oak Tree down yonder
Em   D   C   D
Blow like Hell and bring down Thunder
    Em   D   C   D
And when your raging's through
   Em   D   Em
I'll cut that Oak in two

The Wind began to moan
The old Oak Tree began to groan
Thunder raged like Hell's own daughter
The Air was filled with Fire and Water
And laughing viciously
Lightning struck that tree

The old Oak Tree began to shudder
But he held his ground like some old soldier
His ancient pride was burnt and shaken
But something deep inside did waken
He raised his limbs just like Moses
And blossomed roses
He blossomed roses

Instrumental:
Am, Bm, C, Bm (3x)
Fm, D, C, D, Em

The Sky is clear, the Air is clean
The Earth is brown, the Forest green
The ancient Oak, he still is standing
With strength that passes understanding
Like dreams a noble mind composes
He blossoms roses
He blossoms roses

Recorded on "Roses"
Hayes Court Music/Irving Music

Saturday Night and Sunday Morning

This is one of the first songs I wrote after moving to Nashville. Townes Van Zandt's songs really had an influence on me and I can hear that in this song. There's a YouTube video of Steve Earle doing "Saturday Night and Sunday Morning", which is beautiful. A Dutch DJ, Jan Donkers, used this song on his show for several years. Listening to this now, I can feel myself reaching for a new way to write my songs and express my thoughts and emotions. To me it is neither sad nor joyful, but it is full of life in a quiet thoughtful way. I use a religious image, the water into wine, in the last verse not as a personal statement but as a way to describe the yearning of the singer for his love. When you're in love, religion takes a back seat.

Saturday Night and Sunday Morning

Capo on third fret

```
C        F       C       F               C
If I were Saturday night and you were Sunday morning
     G                              C
For a fleeting moment we could touch at midnight
     G                          C
And in that moment could you really know me
          F           C   F         C
But I am looking 'cross the river longing to be near
     Am        F          C
The water is too wide, I cannot reach you
       G                    C
I'm as close as I can ever hope to be
```

If I was Winter dying and you the virgin Spring
Gladly to your warmth I would surrender
To melt the snows and set the rivers free
But I am standing on the mountain longing to be near
Heaven is too high, I cannot reach you
I'm as close as I can ever hope to be

If you were the water that He turned into wine
And you could satisfy a drunkard's thirst
I'd surely drink until I could not see
But I am lost in the Devil's storm, longing to be near
The wind, it blows too hard, I cannot reach you
I'm as close as I can ever hope to be

If I were Saturday night and you were Sunday
morning For a fleeting moment we could touch at
midnight And in that moment could you really know
me

Recorded on "Eye of the Storm"
Three Minute Movie Music

Sunset on Sunset Boulevard

In my mind, "the sweet young thing with grand ambitions" is played by Marilyn Monroe or Lana Turner. "The handsome face, the youthful body" – Montgomery Clift. The fat man is either Orson Welles or Sidney Greenstreet, or maybe Victor Buono. The aging star could be Joan Crawford or Bette Davis. The narrator/private eye is either Robert Mitchum or Humphrey Bogart. Or me.

The melody and chord progression are more complex than anything else I've written. I had to lay down after I came up with this one. It's dark and moody but also somehow elegant and almost classical. My favorite version of this is on my "Film Noir CD." Jack Irwin's playing and orchestrations are beautiful.

Sunset On Sunset Boulevard

Capo on fifth fret

Intro: Am, Fdim, Am, Fdim, Am, E, Am

```
Am                      Esus   E     A7                          Dm     Fm6
The sweet young thing with grand ambitions,      she's going to be a star one day
                         Am    Esus                                        E
So sweet, so young, so pure, so innocent,      unless you're standing in her way
   Am                      Esus  E, A7                       Dm       Fm6
The handsome face, the youthful body      He made himself a fool proof plan
                         Am    Esus                          E      Am
He'd like to think that he was cheated,      but you can't cheat an honest man
          Fdim  Am              Fdim     Am
That's how it goes,      this case is closed
          E        Am
Sunset on Sunset Boulevard
```

The aging star sips her martini then throws the glass at her TV
"Those filthy swine have all forgotten. How dare they turn their backs on me?"
The fat man slips into his hot tub satisfied, his lust is spent
A thousand bucks to ease the tension, just one more business expense
The sky still glows, but this case is closed
Sunset on Sunset Boulevard

```
G  C                        B      Bm                        A
   I'd like to thank God for my Oscar      but most of all I thank you fans
Am                          Esus E
   I love you because you love me
                              Am
   God bless you all, God bless you all
```

The sirens' wail fades in the distance, they've washed the bloodstains off the
floor The damning photographs have vanished, the body's safely in the morgue
Now there's an opening at the escort service, if you don't mind exotic tastes
The hours are good, the work is easy, don't let this chance go to waste
On goes the show, but this case is closed
Sunset on Sunset Boulevard

   La la la...

Now the farce is finally over, our tawdry drama's at an end
The players soon will be forgotten, there's no more reason to pretend
A cheap hotel, a shot of whiskey, a neon sign like a ragged nerve
A one way ticket to oblivion, we only get what we deserve
Everyone knows this case is closed
Sunset on Sunset Boulevard

Recorded on "Real Lies" and "Film Noir"
David Olney Songs/BMG Bumblebee

Titanic

Level I: an ultra-modern ocean liner crashes into an iceberg and sinks. Sixteen hundred passengers drown. Moral: human arrogance has once again led to tragedy.

Level II: an iceberg longing for love and companionship falls in love with an ocean liner. The iceberg anticipates meeting the beloved with a solemn and eerie passion. Moral: the real dramas of the universe unfold with humans totally unaware of their meaning.

Level III: tragically mismatched lovers are drawn to each other. They can't avoid the catastrophic meeting no matter how they try. Once they meet they can't separate. They are doomed. Moral: always wear a life jacket.

Titanic

No capo
Intro: Em, G, A, G, Em

Em   G   A   G   Em
I am the very heart of this bitter northern sea
                 G   A   G   Em
I've waited in the dark for near eternity
              D   C   D   Em
I am your ancient lover with a love as real as stone
              G   A   G   Em
My frozen arms are reaching, they reach for you alone
Em   Em7   A   C
Come to me Come to me Come to me
  Em
Titanic

The moon and the stars rule the tides and the seasons
Your captain's at the bar, he's drinking with good reason
He raises up his glass and toasts his own disaster
The hallways of the sea are ringing with his laughter
Come to me
Come to me
Come to me
Titanic

The silent current moves and brings us always closer
Tonight, my love, we'll meet and the waiting will be over
I am your ancient lover with a love as real as stone
My frozen arms are reaching
They reach for you alone
Come to me
Come to me
Come to me
Titanic

Come to me
Come to me
Come to me
Titanic

Recorded on "Eye of the Storm" and "Live at Norm's River Road House, Vol. 1"
Red Lilly Music

Vincent's Blues

A tour that was supposed to happen in Holland fell through and I was stuck in Amsterdam. Not a bad city to be stuck in as it turns out. I thought I'd visit the van Gogh Museum. I spent the day checking out his paintings then went back to the hotel. I planned to go to another museum the next day but a voice in my head said to go back to the van Gogh Museum. For the next two days I looked at Vincent's paintings. The last day I took a notebook and stood in front of different works and wrote a verse to go with no particular painting. When I was getting on the train to leave Amsterdam I saw a woman putting her young son on the train. He was about 10 years old. The mother was waving from the platform, a little sad but proud of her boy. He waved back at her, unafraid and ready to see the world.

Vincent's Blues

Capo on third fret

```
A                           D                    A
It's a deep, deep feeling     you can feel time ticking by
          D                              A
There's a child on a train waving to his mama goodbye
        E                        F#m
He's going to see the world
            D           A
Before the world passes by
```

The stars are shining bright with a light that never ends
Every man's a stranger, every stranger is a friend
Vincent knows the feeling
He's been talking to the wind

I walked all night in the rain, there wasn't nothing else to do
All night in the rain and I wore out these walking shoes
But I never seen a thing
Til I seen Vincent with the blues

There's a wind across the wheat field, you can see the sparrow fly
The flowers in the vase are enough to make you cry
How did Vincent get that blue?
He stole it from the sky

You can moan about Monet and get silly about Cezanne
You can rave about Renoir or go crazy about Gauguin
But if you want to see the blues
Ah, Vincent he's your man

It's a deep, deep feeling you can feel time ticking by
There's a child on a train waving to his mama goodbye
He's going to see the world
Before the world passes by

Recorded on "High, Wide and Lonesome" and "Lenora"
David Olney Songs

Wait Here For The Cops

Another "X-Rays" staple. But I don't feel I got to the bottom of the song until I started playing it with Sergio Webb. Sergio's guitar replicates the sound of a police siren during the instrumental break. Hair-raising.

By 1980, I had screwed up enough times to have earned a lifetime exemption from ever seizing the moral high ground. That's what this song is about.

Wait Here For The Cops

No capo

Am
When you live it day after day
        Bb   C   Am
It don't scare you, not like it used to

When you see it, the blood on your hands
        Bb   C   Am
It don't move you, not like it ought to
 G   D   Am
I know what I've done
  G D   Am
But I, I just can't run
         G   D   E
When the running starts it never stops
                  Am
I'm gonna wait here for the cops

I was younger, I was wild, wild
It didn't matter, not like it could have
I was reckless night after night
I didn't care, maybe I should have
Passion and desire, I was burning with a fire
The fire raged, then the fire stopped
I'm gonna wait here for the cops

When your good friend, the one that you trust
Betrays you, that's expected
'Cause the money, he thinks is his share
Comes up short, you're suspected
It's too hot to be this cold
I'm too young to be this old

  G   D Am
I want you all to understandThis ain't a gun
       D   Am
It's my life in my hands
        G   D   E
I'm gonna stay here until I drop
                Am
I'm gonna wait here for the cops

Recorded on "Contender" and "Live At Norm's River Road House, Vol. 1"
Mighty Mighty Music

Walk Downtown

I met a guy at a jam session at a bar in Rowley, Massachusetts. He was the most mild-mannered person you could imagine. Total milquetoast. Then he got on stage to sing a couple of songs with the band and became a rock 'n' roll beast. He finished singing and left the stage and reverted back to his unassuming self. It was shocking to me at the time. I thought of that guy when I wrote the song. I was later to watch myself make the same transformation countless times in countless places. I guess I believe that if you don't transform in some way when you go on stage, then you shouldn't be on stage at all.

Walk Downtown

Capo on third fret
Sixth string tuned down to D

D   G
If I had me a dollar, maybe three or four
       A   D
I might take a little walk downtown, see what they built it for
                   G   D
See what they built it for, see what they built it for
B   A
I might take a little walk downtown
                             D
See what they built it for

I wouldn't walk too long, I wouldn't walk too far
I'd find me a joint with a juke and a seat at the bar
And a seat at the bar, and a seat at the bar
I'd find me a joint with a juke
And a seat at the bar

I might have a drink, I might have me two
If it loosens up my tongue I'll tell the world what you put me
through What you put me through, what you put me through
If it loosens up my tongue I'll tell the world
What you put me through

With the change from a dollar I'll throw a quarter in the juke
I might take me a notion to dance if the barmaid's cute
If the barmaid's cute, if the barmaid's cute
I might take me a notion to dance
If the barmaid's cute

And if the gettin' gets good I might have to sing
You know there ain't nobody better than me impersonating the King
Impersonating the King, impersonating the King
You know there ain't nobody better than me
Impersonating the King

You know I can be found at home alone
If you can't come around, please telephone
Please telephone, please telephone
I got a biga biga hunka hunka love
Viva Las Vegas

If I had me a dollar, maybe three or four
I might take a little walk downtown see what they built it for

Recorded on "High, Wide and Lonesome"
David Olney Songs

When the Deal Goes Down

We were loading the gear in for an X-Rays' gig in Chapel Hill, North Carolina when I was hit by a red pickup truck driven by a guy on his way to the burning pits of hell. I was laid up for a month. I wrote the lyrics with my left hand because my right one was in a cast. It's really an offspring of a Charlie Poole version of "Don't Let Your Deal Go Down." It falls into the category of mad-at-God songs. I thought He or She might appreciate some sage advice from me on how to run the universe. Just trying to be helpful.

Photo by Gregg Roth, additional content by Paul Needham

When The Deal Goes Down

Use capo

Intro: E,G.A,B,A,G,E,G,A,B

```
E                          A
You don't have to lie for me, cry for me or die for me
E                              B
You don't have to fall down on the ground
E                          A
You don't have to give me breath, give me life or give me death
     E         B              E
Just tell me you'll be there when the deal goes down
```

```
                    A
When the deal goes down
                    E
When the deal goes down
      G    A    B         A    G  E     G, A, B
Tell me you'll be there when the deal goes down
```

You don't have to reach for me, pray to me or preach to me
You don't have to make a single sound
You don't have to raise the dead, give me wine or give me bread
Just tell me you'll be there when the deal goes down

When the deal goes down
When the deal goes down
Tell me you'll be there when the deal goes down

You don't have to be the light in the day or in the night
You don't have to wear no heavenly crown
You don't have to save my soul, walk on the water, walk on hot coals
Just tell me you'll be there when the deal goes down

When the deal goes down
When the deal goes down
Tell me you'll be there when the deal goes down

Recorded on "When the Deal Goes Down"
Red Lilly Music

You Never Know

I play this song only using the bottom three strings of the guitar - a fact of which I am inordinately proud, as if I were getting away with something. I took the guitar lick in the first line, "just cause she smiles don't mean she likes you..." to John Hadley and we knocked this one out in a few hours. John Hadley is a painter of some renown. He taught at the University of Oklahoma for a few years. He left there to write songs and routines for the Smothers Brothers. His songs have been recorded by Garth Brooks, Tricia Yearwood, and the Dixie Chicks among others. I am lucky to have him as a co-writer and a friend.

You Never Know

No capo
Sixth string tuned down to D

D
Just 'cause she smiles
Don't mean she likes you
Just 'cause she growls
Don't mean she'll bite
Yeah, she's wild
But is she psycho
You never know
You never know

Is she for real?
Is she just playing?
Is she a rumor?
Is she a fact?
Is she smoke?
Smoke and mirrors?
You never know
You never know

G
  You let her get inside your mind
D
  Now she's in there all the time
G
  You never know til you scratch that itch
Bb   A
  And walk across that burning bridge

        D
Is she the cure?
The doctor ordered
For the fever
In your brain?
Is this Paris?
Or is this Newark?
You never know
You never know

Recorded on "Dutchman's Curve"
Red Lilly Music/Hadley Six Music

CPSIA information can be obtained
at www.ICGtesting.com
Printed in the USA
LVOW05s0223090516
487275LV00007B/21/P